EMERALD BREATH

Poems to Foster Beauty
cosetta romani

Emerald Breath: Poems to Foster Beauty
Cosetta Romani

Copyright ©2016 by Cosetta Romani
All rights reserved, including the right to reproduce this
work in any form whatsoever, without permission
in writing from the author, except in brief passages
in connection with a review.

Cover design by NXT Creates
Cover art by Paul Paladin c/o iStock.com
Interior book design by NXT Creates

Printed in the United States of America

ISBN 978-1539737728

For Ivo
*My Beloved Consort and Soul Mate of many lifetimes.
With you Life is more Alive.*

GRATITUDE

My foremost gratitude goes to Life Itself, breathing, beating, expressing, and shaping as me, as you, as them, in forms and formlessness.

I am especially grateful to:

- *Char Sundust* for journeying to my heart and finding the inner poet waiting to be hatched.

- *Sierra Nelson*, the editor I needed at this stage of my writing. She didn't change or bruise my work with a mere dry critique. Instead, her tender and gentle nature invited me to further inquiring. In only few meetings I grew and learned immensely.

- *Audra Brown* from nxtcreates.com who designed this book like a magic tailor and blesses me every day with her friendship.

- *Zahra Sedghinasb, Lisa Cooper, Pamela Roberson* for being amazing buddies to write with. I will always treasure our evening writing circles and the love and support we gave to one another.

- *Julie McGene* for her friendship, good judgment and valuable feedback.

- *All my teachers and students* who, over the years, praised my voice and the wisdom coming through. You encouraged me to print my learning on paper.

- Last but not least to *my precious husband Ivo Grossi*, who was the first to listen to each poem multiple times with the ear of an editor and the heart of a lover.

FORWARD

As I write the foreword to *Emerald Breath* – Poems to foster beauty – I am reminded of the privilege I had in being there with Cosetta, either on the scene or as first receiver, while she was capturing into poetry the images created by the reflection of her heart, beaming light onto the canvass of life.

You are about to enter a heart of beauty, sensuality, depth and lightness.

Emerald Breath pulls open the curtain of mind and lets the natural world shine through. The natural elements, the trees, the rose, the lilies, the turtle, the robin, the boa, the heron, the crow, the moon, the sun and the river, they all become pregnant with Shakti. They share their unspoken wisdom. They bestow their beauty. They teach their inner dimensions.

This poetry carries the power of the shamanic journey.

Be prepared for your habitual mental lenses to melt. Be open for *Emerald Breath* to whisper straight into your heart the hidden beauty of the natural world. Simply feel and bask in its divine light.

Ivo Grossi
Yoga and meditation teacher, shamanic practitioner

INTRODUCTION

When I was a young girl I was gifted with a beautiful red dairy. What I really liked about it was the lock and the tiny key attached to its hard cover. I called it "diario segreto," secret diary.

At the end of each day, I would sit on my bed, insert the key to unlock the diary and enter it like a secret garden. I wrote with my whole body, breathing, wandering and getting lost inside the young blossoms of my inner landscape. I wrote details of my ordinary discoveries with gusto. I confessed and asked for help without holding back.

Writing was a way to meet the friend within myself and together imagine stories bigger than us. I took refuge in the writing for many years to come. But I also stopped writing for as many years. The less I wrote, the less I felt the desire to write, until eventually I abandoned the ritual.

Then, on a day in 2005, during an intuitive reading with a medicine woman who became my mentor for a long time, I was struck by her message. She said to me: "Cosetta, you have a poet living in your heart who is dying. I urge you to find a writing coach right away to unlock this expansive energy and free the poet!"

And so I did.

Writing became a vital practice to rescue this being in my heart, and poetry came to life. Today I write poems to cultivate awareness of the extraordinary fleeting moments. It helps me to be present instead of letting the moment slip by unnoticed.

The key is to pay attention and use all my senses to unlock the secrets and unveil the beauty of each instant. I know that with practice this inclination to see all moments this way will strengthen.

English is not my mother tongue but a second language I began learning in 2000, when I left Italy to move to Seattle, with a one-way ticket in my hands and frisson in my heart. It is a challenging and a beautiful exploration that allows me to play with the gems of this language.

May these poems sigh to your heart and free you to see the moving beauty of your life.

Cosetta Romani
Seattle, November 2016

CONTENTS

Invocation	1
Saraswathi	2
Rose	3
Red Poppies	5
Leaf	8
Ask a Tree	10
Purple Lilies	14
Perfection	16
Crow	17
Meeting	19
Boa Initiation	20
Ode to a Robin	22
Heron	24
Tortuga Blanca	26
Forest	28
Cedar Cleansing	30
Supplication to the Wind	31
Autumn	32
Nowness	34
River	35
Daily Refuge	36
To My Writing Muse	38
Today's Special	40
Ocean Love	42
Sun	44
Clouds	46
Conversation with the Moon	48
The Labor of Poetry	50

INVOCATION

Emerald breath
now
opening
emptying
deepening.

Emerald breath
where
life happens.

Emerald breath
now.

SARASWATHI

Today I choose the path of broken heart,
face to face
hand in hand
with the Goddess living in me.

She is the white tulip
sleeping on the altar.

She undulates along
the river of my blood.

She is the silk of grace
in my inspired thinking.

She lives at the roots
of my silence
and rises to sit on my tongue
to bless the words I speak,
sing and write.

She waters my prayers.

We ride and rest on two giant swans:
the white for the day
the black for those brave nights
when time comes to go inside
the dark unafraid.

ROSE

That moment mattered!

When these eyes captured
the pearls of dew around your neck
and the jolly fingers of the morning wind
opening your red robe...

just enough petals to show me
the unblemished spiral
of your essence.

When I place my nose on your velvety lips
you speak first
with an intense perfumed tongue
of unrivaled love.

Is this why you have existed long before humans?
Is this why you are the favored flower
at the feet of the Source?
Is this why you are at the heart of all hearts?

I want to stay longer with you,
unfold together
to the beauty of this morning,
but all I can do is a pause,
brief like a butterfly,

then move on the next thing to do
hoping you will stay
as you are
when I return.

Instead you quietly expand.
By the time I turn back
to glance at you,
you have offered
all your petals to the sun
and the spiral is gone.

RED POPPIES

In the early morning,
while my body resists
the impulse of stretching out
and pulling on
the new day,
they open.

A small family of
bright
weightless fire
on tall green hairy legs
wafts softly
with the summer breeze.

Oh my scarlet friends,
I have been waiting for
your elegant blossoms
a year.
And now you are
gone tomorrow,
or the day after.

Your short-lived
fleeting splendor
urges me to simplify,

to release old stories
I am still rehearsing
to the ground
with your petals.
I begin fresh,
look at your black heart
exposed liked mine,
and introduce a new self
to my Self.

We are bulging stars
filled with ripening seeds
of goodness.

People have been using
your medicine
for centuries to
numb wounds,
sleep good,
delight food.

You had the courage to bloom
in trench warfare
while getting blood-stained.
You became the death stone
for many.
Would I have been as brave as you?

We both live on the same land,
we need water and sunlight to flourish,
we help each other,
what a kinship is this!

At sunset light
I will water the garden,
check and guess
which of you
will toss first
a wrinkled skirt.

I know you will pretend
to be dormant.

In the early morning,
while my mind confuses
sleeping with waking,
a new opium
arises to life.

A poppy awakes
sunlight intakes
and so do I.

LEAF

Soaring
Slender
Green

Undulation on
the rims
softening the void.

I look at you
and hear your swift whisper
please buy me.

I remove you from the cluttered bucket,
for if no one else sees you the way I do
you may decay here.

Dominating figure of softness
you will pass soon
like all things that have life,

but now
I let my eyes draw a new
form of you
and my hands
place your stature
inside a curled iron frame.

I arrange a society of orange
and yellow blossoms
at your feet
to emphasize your regalia.

The freshness of this play is my way
to preserve
the experience
of this moment.

ASK A TREE

Ask a cedar, a maple, an olive tree
how to stand strong when
the winds of loss
will whip you down.

Ask a redwood,
a eucalyptus, or a palm tree
how to grow taller than
your disappointments.

Ask a chestnut, a cherry,
a jungle tree how to lean
into light and grow
slanting arms of love.

Ask a blooming tree
about the beauty
of your bearing
stillness.

Ask conifers
how to preserve
your gifts and talents
all year round.

Ask an alder tree
how you can bridge
your need to root
and flow.

Ask large-bodied trees
how to halt
your doing
and rest in being.

Ask the forest about
the freedom of diversity
and the power
of its oneness.

Ask any tree how
to let go of your need to know
and whirl like leaves
with death's wind.

Ask a log
how to burn
for others
with such love.

Ask a tree
all your questions.
Then wait.

Wait.

Wait.

PURPLE LILIES

A bouquet of
pregnant goddesses,
their wombs
wrapped around
hidden love.

I please them with
a regal vase
on a luminous
cool corner
of the kitchen countertop.

I am captivated by their
exotic presence,
mostly by the slow
unfurling
silent labor.

I watch their bellies,
wanting to catch
that movement,
that tremor,

I can't
unless
I let my feet
become
still like stems.

Time goes by,
their bellies expand.
I exalt at the first
explosive sprout...

One by one,
six wine purple arms
curling a bow,
knowing that
life moves
below their eyes.

In the center there is
a heart unhurt,
intoxicated by its own beauty
and open to the flow of time.

PERFECTION

*Written on an Alaska aircraft
on Thanksgiving Day*

I cross the sky
on a man-made craft,
eyes leveled with
the glow of God.

I blink
Slowly
not to disturb
the birth of dawn,

a supreme triumph
over raw white
cotton clouds.

I receive the embrace.

CROW

I walk
walk
walk
to undress a mind
restlessly thinking,
beneath this going
a naked longing for
stillness.

You caw
caw
caw
a new song from
the mystery
like a spell
from a wand
to halt me.

Only when I roost on
the empty log
across from you
your beak clamped shut
eyes fixing me like stone
time seems pausing.

You see you have
moved me to presence
then fly free on ebony wings
as if that was the only reason
we had to meet.

Now, dressed with stillness,
I have no desire of going,
I stay.

MEETING

Clouds float following the wind,
space opens to light bearing crystal air.
I walk on a desolate beach the long shore is vast.
An assembly of crows, seagulls and pigeons
scavenging human food on the open ground.
Sounds interwoven with silence,
actions synchronized with the ocean's breath.
I squat on my heels a fashionable perch.
I become the avian winging toward
magnificent mountains, random perfection.
I land on the crest meeting heaven and earth.
Humbled alight into gratitude.

BOA INITIATION

It was fear at first sight.

I've often wondered about
the temperature of your body,
the texture of your skin.

A nonpoisonous constrictor
raised and loved like a pet
in the same room with me.
Am I ready for this?

Ten feet of thick length, thirty pounds
of enormous frame,
carrying many live creatures inside.

Beautiful is your golden body,
mystical are the tribal markings,
a cryptic language of jagged lines,
circles, ovals and diamonds.

I let my arms branch out:
you found your way around,
and it was love at first touch.

Your bigness quietly twisting,
lengthening,
contracting
along my skin –

teaching me
how to
shed
all I have
become till now.

New responses to life
raising from
the base of my spine,
my blood a wild river.

You flick your tongue
around my neck,
smelling,
tasting me
like a lover
or a prey.

I open my ears
to your spoken breath
and quiver,
and wake
to a new conversation
with the divine.

Ecstatic in body,
serene in mind,
I think of this moment
as the good one to die.

ODE TO A ROBIN

The Sound of Spring is here.

Its nature does not ask it
to know about seas,
neither of sweet waters –

yet, when springs visit
my backyard,
it behaves like an expert sailor,

balancing with bravery
on the mast's top
of a lively cypress.

It shows up on dreary days
of downpour
or glorious skies

with a loyalty to life
that
I dream to have.

It remains vigilant,
it sings from dawn to dusk
the same rich refrain

that cheers and stirs up
the pool of life
when we let it dry.

Oh Robin,
is your singing
what replenishes you?

I thank you for your brilliance
and give myself
permission to do the same.

HERON

It lands silently
on the rim of the deck
with its long thin legs
bringing back
my forward thinking
to the now.

Its beak points
with precision
inviting me to move closer
than I ever found myself before.

I recognize the privilege
of the encounter
the moment I sit with vigilance
and mirror the stoic presence.

The wise teacher begins to speak
of no action
of highly focused stillness
of upright elegance
of intense tranquility.

My wanting moves below the very water
into which I am gazing,
but I don't chase it
nor expect it.

In silence I see opportunities swim by.
In stillness I feel the tides of true desire.
With patience I learn to choose.
With the rigor of a warrior I strike.

Can you exert this kind of love for attention?

TORTUGA BLANCA

For nights on end
under the last ray of moonlight
I search the sand
for her untouched tracks,
but I am left alone
with pointless traces
– my own –
which I release to
the uncharted swing
of a hammock...

But then
slowly she sails the last wave
dreaming her destiny.
She touches the land
before midnight,
finally meeting
my nights of desire.

A silent moving shadow,
going with purpose
though her finding
is uncertain.

She rows the sand
with great effort,

pulling her soul-case
patiently,
willfully,
in a way I cannot.

The white head
chooses to dig a nest
close to my feet.
I stay motionlessly present
while she lays
one hundred treasures
of translucent white.

Tears of accomplishment
from her ancient eyes
wetting the cracked skin,
deep breaths,
quiet anguish,
a short rest,
serene acceptance,
she knows she will never see
her hatchlings.

I watch her body
tattooing imprints,
mother earth meeting herself.

FOREST

You move me like a feather
with your emerald breath,
quieting my mind like moss.

Now,
an open day
to be discovered.

It feels good to be in the woods.

I allow observation
to show me how to smell,
how to taste, in a new way,
this living song of creation.

I ask you, ancient forest,
how to realign my body, mind and tongue
with all that has true heart and meaning.

The Tree people talk:

"You are in the right place to learn about
the cycle of your life.

Don't try.
Simply stand like we do.
Breathe. Breathe.

Don't waste time,
nor efforts,
to maintain
your sense of self.

Don't resist.
Exist!

You have entered a time
in your growth
where you can risk more
and try less.

Practice boundaries around creativity.

Protect it.
Play with it.
Live it.

Without consistency
you struggle,
you rob yourself, literally,
like a *ladro.**

"Now, go wash your mind in the river."

I bow out,
silenced by
overwhelming gratitude.

* *a thief*

CEDAR CLEANSING

I duck under a majestic cedar tree
and lay down on the lowest branch
weighted down
by a tight sense of separation
knotted with judgment.

With the weapon of my exhalation
I sever the ties
Ahhhh...I am victorious.

With a slow,
deep inhalation
I climb up the branches
cascading over me
to find freedom in the air.

Like all conifers I too depend on wind
to pollinate new ways of being
to grow the seeds embedded
in the sap of my soul.

SUPPLICATION TO THE WIND

Trees still full with less...

Oh Sapient one
that rattles death
I beg you to shake my head
to make a pile
with my disappointments.

Blow me in the air
toss me
nibble on
this busy mind,
then spit out
any poor mentality.

Leave me there
flat and scattered
on the deck
with those dry leaves
until I birth
a new commitment to
plentiful living.

Then breathe me like the first time.

AUTUMN

I amble along Green Lake
and watch
death
dancing
side by side
with what still has life.

Green fading from grasses,
trees shifting their robes:
burgundy,
amaranth,
golden
and bronze.

Some branches at ease
in their nudity, already.

Sudden tears of
laughter dripping
from the sky.

I smell them before
they touch the ground
and become
mossy fragrance.

I raise my chin,
invite my tongue to taste
your faces, Gods, and you ask me:

"Why do you keep contending with death?
When will you learn to let go like leaves do?"

NOWNESS

It is a new day
to step outside with
feet bare
hands empty
jaw unclutched
eyes soft
nostrils open.

I exhale a bow
of reverence
to the dazzling sun
whose presence
purifies
my character
perpetually.

And who else is feeding me
with freshness
while living with old collectibles?

Two hummingbirds
playing acrobats with the sky
for my amusement.

RIVER

The river would be silent
if it didn't meet
the stone people
along the path.

Instead it strikes
marvelous conversations
with stones of all size,
shaping a singing refrain:

Don't hold
Go down
Free flow
Flow now.

I go to the river
to wash my stories
to find stillness
in the movement.

DAILY REFUGE

I look down this old tub deprived of beauty,
too small for my stature.
The wall around it tiled with doleful green,
it is the only thing we didn't change
during a major remodeling. I still wonder why.
Even so I keep it clean and shining.

With my right foot,
the one that always leads
and never injures by distractions,
I take a safe step inside the temple
pull the silky white curtain
sealing the time.

I turn the spout on
and the water gushes instantly
at 101 degrees F.
It is that mixing valve
we installed at the water heater,
the miracle maker.
It saves unnecessary waste
that we modern people
take for granted.

My skin favors this maternal temperature.
I stand open
under the showerhead and
let life stream down my crown,
all the joys and distresses.
I watch my big days becoming small,
whirling down the drain
until nothing remains.
I murmur a prayer of gratitude.

TO MY WRITING MUSE

I read you stand by many
with bottles of ink
whispering.

I see you stand by me
mute,
hidden in a conch.

In the midst of tempests,
when my mind ebbs the heart
of its deep desire to write,
you emerge.

You watch the wrestling
with great amusement,
knowing there is a poem
waiting for life
beneath that swell.

Without your voice
I am prey of
my resistance,
unable to abide
in what is true
and meaningful.

Afraid of silence,
away from patience,
I drop the pen,
abandon the page,
to feed
this starved expression
with food and wine.

Instantly you coil
inside the conch
and move across the sea,
coasting the horizon
of my longing,
patiently waiting
for the wave of my surrender.

TODAY'S SPECIAL

MENU:

Depressed economy
Wars
Global injustice
Unwanted refugees
Environmental disasters,

Served with

Busy minds
Glazed with technology
Free range fear
Aged with devastation
Or
A fresh harvest of love for
Preservation.

Yet
Today's special is:

An unblemished sky
Hosting a golden light ball
Of rounded perfection.

Its stillness
A dynamic reflection
On the dancing ocean.

Waves birthing and dying
Piano, crescendo, forte,
Crushing refrains of water
Meeting the earth.

OCEAN LOVE

Here
at the beach
where the weather

is
always
right,

I find
my breath
growing fuller,

feet
sinking
deeper.

I bow to the ocean
and step on her skirt,
she gives a cold flap

that resurrects
the stream
in my heart.

With long arms
she pulls me closer
to her breasts

to wash the stress
that steals
my zest,

splashing
her giant belly
over my crown

crashing strings of thoughts,
buckets of moods
and shoulds and wrongs.

This water is my mother,
no wonder her tears are
as salty as mine.

SUN

You ascend and
descend alone
like all leaders do.

Humanity worships you,
looking up
like abiding flowers –
or ignores you,
looking down,
wrestling like ants
under your golden robe.

You rise
to burn love
for eons now.
What a star you are!

Spouse to nights
you will never meet.

Lover to a moon
you will never touch.

Sustainer of a grand earth
you feed in tidal swirls.

You know
the order of things
beyond right,
beyond wrong,
and keep rising and loving.

CLOUDS

A cloth of sky flies from this window,

clouds in flight
holding breath
so I can see what they can be,

dark patches

soft wings

of a majestic owl returning west.

A clan of clouds
roaming slow.

Now, large like mountains.
Beams of light underneath
warming,
dissolving gray

while a scarlet source shouts silent colors

to end the day.

CONVERSATION WITH THE MOON

Thickness in motion,
clustering clouds,
you seem to be gone.
Yet you do return
in white bloom
to light my darkness
with your brightness.

You are full, dear moon,
something I care for much.
Time to pay homage to
your tireless cycle
and pray, this month again,
for one more generous healing.

"Are you still drunk with doubts
and old wounds?"
you ask me.
"I keep telling you to go
in and out of
that place of dark gifts
without dwelling there."

I burst out, "I tried, mother,
I tried, but I don't know how,
I am tired and scared."

The moon now howling at my soul,
"What happened doesn't matter,
what you learn from those stories does.
Your mind is crowded with should.
Your body constipated with food.
You are cold with agony.
My daughter, before the night shifts,
redeem your shadows,
free ingrained misconceptions."

I reply, "Yes, please shine on
my ability to see
with white eyes
the best in myself,
my worth, my life.
I want to touch the fragmented Self,
mend those parts that shattered
the instant I judged."

And you do shine
on the entrance of darkness,
and I do enter it
and weave
the broken pieces
back together.

I am received
by my own heart,
and lay down
on the lawn
under your amorous embrace.

THE LABOR OF POETRY

A beach crowded with happiness...

Children digging,
running, squealing.
Parents quieting,
resting, watching.

The air is gentle,
the sky clear,
the sun splendid,
the sand warm.

This beauty brings peace
and also ignites a battle for words.
A poem, its labor
now taking over:

Cold glittering ocean,
eyes riding the moving essence.
I dunk underwater,
spinning alchemical words
of magic, of owe.
I find nothing.

I rise to a new sight,
the mountains of north,
and soar over their shoulders.

Poems are often found
at these tops
or under a rock.

Nothing is here,
only the pain
of my yearning
for writing with glow.

Why hunting for words?
Can I let them roll
like incantations?

I hear the laughter
of palm fronds
and ask them
about a trance-like state
that shuts off my brain
with its need to explain.

They say to pray,
to open my bones
to God, who will
sing through them in prose.

Thus I drop paper and pen,
lay down on the sand,
let God kiss my hand
and empty, empty, empty
under the blue sky.

Photo credit: Thomas Romani

Cosetta Romani was born in Italy and moved to Seattle in 2000 with her husband Ivo and their son Emmanuele. She is a shimmering being, an accomplished teacher and healer whose creative expression is embodied in all she does.

She uses breath work, intuitions, oracles nature, asana, meditations, mantras, visualizations, healing touch, singing, dancing, writing and poetry to feel and connect with the Body, Mind-Heart and Spirit of each student.

You can read more about her at
www.puravitayoga.com

Made in the USA
Middletown, DE
17 December 2016